simple*Solutions*

Bathrooms

simple Solutions

Bathrooms

COLEEN CAHILL

Foreword by Gale C. Steves,
Editor-in-Chief, *Home Magazine*

FRIEDMAN/FAIRFAX
PUBLISHERS

Acknowledgements

I'd like to thank several people for their enthusiasm, insight, and helpful advice: Tim Drew and Gale Steves at *Home Magazine,* Christine Abbate, Timm Brandhorst, Brian and Chris Cahill, Maureen Cahill, and Leslie Gross. And special thanks to Kathleen Wolfe and Sharyn Rosart at Friedman/Fairfax.

A FRIEDMAN/FAIRFAX BOOK
Please visit our website: www.metrobooks.com

© 2001 by Michael Friedman Publishing Group, Inc.

Library of Congress Cataloging-in-Publication Data available upon request.

ISBN 1-56799-928-X

Editor: Sharyn Rosart
Art Director: Jeff Batzli
Photo Editor: Kathleen Wolfe
Production Manager: Richela Fabian Morgan
Design: Lindgren/Fuller Design, Inc.

Color separations by Colourscan Overseas Co Pte Ltd
Printed in Hong Kong by C & C Offset Printing Co., Ltd

10 9 8 7 6 5 4 3 2 1

Distributed by Sterling Publishing Company, Inc.
387 Park Avenue South
New York, NY 10016
Distributed in Canada by Sterling Publishing
Canadian Manda Group
One Atlantic Avenue, Suite 105
Toronto, Ontario, Canada M6K 3E7
Distributed in Australia by
Capricorn Link (Australia) Pty Ltd.
P.O. Box 6651
Baulkham Hills, Business Centre, NSW 2153, Australia

Contents

Foreword

What with shower installations that do everything but make the morning coffee and whirlpool spa tubs guaranteed to hydraulically knead you into relaxed nirvana, we seem to have entered a golden age of bathroom accoutrements and design. This great leap forward makes it all the more difficult to believe that not so terribly long ago, the luxury of a fully equipped bathroom was exactly that—a luxury. And even once it had become commonplace in the average home, beyond basic function, little thought was given to bath design. A perfect object lesson to consider is that in the 1920s, a new two-story, three-bedroom middle-class house might well have included only one full bath upstairs and a tiny powder room downstairs. That so-called full bath was just big enough to accommodate a tub, a pedestal sink, and a toilet. A mirrored medicine cabinet provided all the storage you needed, provided you had nothing more than a few toiletries, a bottle each of aspirin and iodine, and some Band-Aids. Somehow, this was deemed entirely adequate for a family of four to six. Whose concept of comfort was this, and what were they thinking? Did anyone consider what a bottleneck this would be as everyone tried to get ready in the morning?

Technology and bathroom design have, thank goodness, come a very long way since then. Ergonomic researchers and thoughtful designers have joined forces to bring about a revolution in comfort, utility, and safety. When it comes to the seemingly simple act of bathing, for example, we now have choices that would nonplus our grandparents. For showering, we can choose all manner of variations, from handheld to adjustable-flow massaging showerheads to multiple body sprays. Or we can combine them—and perhaps add a steam unit—for what bath-fixture manufacturers might call the "ultimate showering experience." Of course, when decompressing from a stressful day is the goal, a long, hot, soothing soak in a whirlpool tub can be just what the doctor ordered. What would probably most astound our grandparents is that all of these elements are available at affordable prices.

Except perhaps the kitchen, no other room in the house will demand so many decisions and offer so little leeway for changing your mind. Moving plumbing lines and fixture sites is appreciably more difficult and expensive than rearranging the furniture in the living room. And there's so much to consider: fixtures, fittings, lighting, and ventilation. Oh, and besides all that, how should it look? Do you want ceramic tile, stone, or a man-made solid-surfacing material? And then, there are also safety and maintenance issues to contend with.

If you're daunted by the size of the task, just close your eyes and think back to every steamy, clammy, mildewed, ill-lit, cold-floored, cluttered, wet towel-strewn bathroom you've ever had the pleasure of meeting and realize that there has to be a better way. In the following pages, you'll find a wealth of inspiration to help you get started on finding your own better way.

Gale C. Steves
Editor-in-Chief
Home Magazine

Introduction

The bathroom is one of the most personal and functional rooms in the home. That wasn't always the case. In fact, the bathroom didn't start out as an indoor member of the family at all. Outhouses, chamber pots, and basins for washing were the conveniences of the day until the plumbing moved indoors. Since then, the bathroom has gone through many incarnations before arriving at the lavish amenity-filled retreats of today.

In the early part of the twentieth century, the focus on the bathroom was as a functional space. Bathrooms were generally small, and not much attention was paid to how the room looked. Typically, three critical fixtures—the sink (known as a lavatory in the industry), tub, and toilet—were arranged in a utilitarian manner that took up minimal space. However, things began to change in the 1920s and '30s, when the idea to incorporate more decorative elements became popular. This was a time of great style, and the bathroom began to reflect the look of the rest of the home.

After World War II, as suburbs blossomed, the bathroom became an important consideration in newly constructed homes. More square footage was devoted to bathrooms than ever before. Many new homes could now boast a powder room, comfortable master bath, and second full bath designed for the children. The interest in decorating bathrooms had firmly taken root, and colorful tiles and fixtures appeared in a thoroughly modern palette of colors.

This increased focus on the bathroom ultimately led to innovation. The most notable innovation was a tub with water jets introduced by Roy Jacuzzi in 1968. During the next two decades, the popularity of whirlpools soared. The size of bathrooms, especially master baths, followed suit. Many adults began looking at their bathrooms as places to relax and pamper themselves. This trend continues today, as does the demand for new and innovative bathroom solutions.

Bathrooms continue to be at the top of remodeling lists for both full-scale renovations and minor facelifts. Investing in your bathroom makes good economic sense. Along with the kitchen, it is one of the showcase rooms that adds significant value to your home—and enjoyment to your daily life.

The recent explosion in diverse materials and bathroom fixtures available has made planning any bathroom a significant undertaking. The best place to start your planning is with a review of your entire family's needs. Consider how those needs may change in the future. For instance, many families find that when their kids become teenagers, an extra shower comes in handy. This often leads to renovating a downstairs powder room to include a stall shower. An alternative that's gaining in popularity is to skip the powder room in the front of the house altogether and plan for a full bath in the back of the house.

Regardless of the bathroom you're planning, whether a traditional powder room or full family bath, there are practical issues that must be addressed. Moisture and ventilation are two important concerns, and the materials used in the bathroom must stand up to the rigors of daily use. Adequate storage will contribute to an efficient bathroom and should also be considered upfront. Beyond these basics, there are a host of decisions that only you can make: One sink or two in the master bath? Do you need a shower and a tub? How far do you go in tailoring a bathroom to the needs and tastes of children?

There is more than one solution to every bathroom question, which is why *Simple Solutions: Bathrooms* is filled with ideas and tips that will inspire you to create the kind of bathrooms that will work for your entire family. After all, as the first room we visit in the morning and the last we see before we say good night, the bathroom occupies a unique place in the home.

Coleen Cahill

Powder Rooms

Form and function: today's powder rooms promise both. The traditional powder room, typically found in the front of the house, is the most public of a home's bathrooms, and therefore is a good place to focus on style. You can extend the decorating themes of the main rooms or experiment with a completely new look. For those homes that would benefit from a more functional powder room, consider adding a bath or shower; if you're ready for a bigger change, perhaps move the room to the back of the house.

bright ideas

- Splurge on marble, granite, or dazzling mosaic floors
- Make a statement with an untraditional sink
- Hang an antique mirror
- Highlight walls with decorative painting effects

This powder room uses stone to beautiful effect. The washbasin is a modern interpretation of the centuries-old washstand and is set on a deep shelf that takes the place of a traditional vanity. ➲

Bowl washbasins like this one are available in a variety of materials, from glass to chrome; they make a strong decorative statement.

An integral metal sink makes a sleek statement. Its rectangular shape and unusual bowl add an industrial touch to this powder room. ☊

A classic pedestal sink is an ideal choice for this small powder room. The simple color scheme and minimal décor work together to make the most of the space. Note how the traditional black-and-white tiled floor draws together the sink, mirror, and wall sconces. A shallow glass shelf just above the sink offers a bit of open storage. ➲

A wide lip on a sink is more than decorative: it can accomodate washing amenities, a vase, or a stack of guest towels.

A non-traditional sink and vanity are the focal point of this stylishly modern powder room. The multihued tile backsplash is a fitting backdrop for the asymmetric sink and complements the warm wood tones of the vanity. ◓

Decorative sconces flanking the mirror provide necessary light and enhance the style of the room.

In this next-generation powder room, enlarged to include a shower, a minimal approach to the décor results in a clean, calm look for a functional space. White subway tiles and chrome are durable choices that look fresh while standing up to daily use; a subtly printed wallpaper above the molding softens the look. ↻

Mirrors reflect the light in this airy powder room. Simple, stylish, and functional, the room features an oversized vanity that offers ample storage and a sleek countertop and undermounted sink. ⌒

A corner sink and vanity are great space-saving solutions—especially for a smaller powder room. Style does not need to be sacrificed to space, as this gleaming copper basin and faucet fitted into a curved pine vanity prove. ◑

Shallow cabinets provide sleek, unexpected storage.

In this stylish powder room, a traditional vanity is replaced by a sculptural pedestal upon which rests a metal washbasin. The mix of materials—stone, metal, and wood—combine with the varied forms to create a modern effect. ➲

Small Spaces

Bathrooms often get squeezed into small or awkward spaces, raising the question: How can you make sure you get **everything** you need into a limited space? Planning is the key. Start experimenting on paper or computer before you commit to fixtures. And don't forget to think creatively about **storage**. If there's one thing that can make a small bathroom seem spacious, it's the ability to keep clutter out of the way.

bright ideas

- Pedestal sinks with integral towel bars and/or generous set-down areas
- Glass shower doors
- A space-saving corner sink/vanity
- Built-in recessed storage

There's room for a large shower in this small bathroom and, thanks to the glass wall/shower door, it still feels open and airy. Another good idea is the recessed medicine cabinet, which yields storage without protruding into the room. ➲

The vanity's integral sink-countertop extends over the toilet to create a useful additional shelf.

A small niche below the medicine cabinet provides a convenient place for hand towels and serves as a perfect display perch—proving that storage can be stylish as well as functional. 🎧

Built-ins make this small bath an extremely functional space. A shallow ledge at the foot of the tub was designed to hold soaps and shampoos while a tidy niche on the opposite wall stores a supply of fresh towels. ⌒

An oversized pedestal sink relieves any feeling of being cramped by providing plenty of elbow and leg room. ➲

A simple design scheme uses stunning black-veined marble on the floor and walls to unify the small space.

A mirror along one wall makes a narrow room seem wider.

This galley-style bathroom squeezes a lot of storage into a narrow space. The vanity and countertop extend the full length of the room, creating both hidden storage and surface space, while a chome baker's rack provides easy access to towels. ☾

When space is an issue, a combination whirlpool bath/shower like this one is a clever solution. It offers many of the same features found in much larger home spas. An added bonus: built-in shelves help keep toiletries organized. ☋

A bidet is fitted next to the toilet, making the most of the room's narrow dimensions.

Decorative details can be used to make a small room seem larger. Here, an old window has been turned into a mirror that offers a "view" that expands the room through its reflection. ⋂

Recessed drawers flanking the center cabinet provide convenient storage without protruding into the room.

A well-designed vanity provides plenty of storage and counter space without overwhelming this small bathroom. The vanity's floating design enhances the sense of space. ⚲

Ceramic wall tiles in a golden hue protect the area around the tub and are extended throughout the room, lending it visual coherence. ⊂

Several solutions "enlarge" this small bathroom: a vaulted ceiling helps the tight space feel more open, while the window above the tub lets in light and draws the eye to the outdoors. A metal washbasin is an ideal choice, offering a stylish and space-saving solution. ⊃

Simplicity is the key to making a small space feel roomy. In this case, a shower was passed over in favor of a luxurious tub. That's a purely personal decision, but it's worth considering if space is limited. ↻

A narrow shelf above the mosaic tile work encircles the room.

Mirrored sliding doors disguise additional storage and make the room appear larger.

This small guest bathroom combines style, function, and comfort. A slim pedestal sink is an ideal choice when space is limited; wall-mounted accessories, including a towel bar, soap dish, and cup holder, keep items accessible and minimize clutter. ☊

Glass shower doors are a smart choice for small bathrooms because the sight line remains uninterrupted. The vertical orientation of the large rectangular tiles is another space-enhancing tactic, as the tiles draw the eye up and toward the decorative border. ➲

Kids Only

 Kid-friendly baths come in all shapes and sizes. Good design will help keep the bathroom **safe** for young children and careful planning will ensure that it **grows** with them. (Think teenagers!) How far you want to go in tailoring a bathroom to suit your kids depends on both personal taste and budget.

bright ideas

- Pullout step under vanity
- Lower-height countertops
- Showerheads/ faucets with anti-scald controls
- Illuminated light switches
- Non-slip rubber-backed bath mats

This room abounds with kid-safe features such as the "soft" bathtub made of a supple and slip-resistant material that cushions any falls. Walls and floor are also slip-resistant—and easy to wipe clean. ➲

Anti-scald plumbing fittings keep hot water at a safe temperature, and the whimsical hand shower is easy for kids to handle. 🎧

Hooks are hung at the perfect height for kids. Note the step stool, an easy solution until kids are tall enough to reach the sink on their own.

This space easily accommodates kids yet has great growth potential. The all-white room is accented with primary colors for now, but that can easily change as kids grow. 🎧

- ☐ Integral and under-mounted sinks for easy clean-up
- ☐ Non-slip surfaces for floor and shower stall
- ☐ Rounded corners on vanity tops, countertop edges, and cabinet doors
- ☐ Floor drain for toilet or tub overflows

Pretty custom tiles that frame the window above the bath were the only indulgence in this modest design.

For a twelve-year old girl who wanted a grown-up bathroom, coordinated products from Home Depot were an affordable solution. The vanity, in an anodized indigo stain, has a solid-surface counter at adult height (to grow into) and offers plenty of storage for now and the future. ◑

A bathroom designed just for grandchildren is a well-considered success. Two sinks are the best way to keep kids out of each other's way, and at 30 inches (75cm)—which is six inches (15cm) shorter than standard—they are a kid-friendly height. ☝

Pigeonhole cubbies and drawers are coded for each of the four grandchildren by the color of the knobs. Towels are color-coordinated, too. ☝

Soccer ball faucets add a playful touch, and appeal to girls and boys alike.

Simple accessories like this overflow-drain cover both protect children and discourage tampering with the bath. ➲

Hooks are an excellent solution for children young and older, for whom towel racks often seem to represent quite a challenge. Hooks come in a wide range of styles to suit every bathroom— and even the peel-and-stick variety come in handy. ↻

Bright towels pick up on the colorful accent tiles, making this bath fun for kids. A convenient towel rack with shelf above helps keep bath things organized—a plastic basket is a simple solution for smaller items. ◖

Shared by three teenagers, this bathroom possesses an old-fashioned charm thanks to a reproduction claw-foot bathtub and old-style hardware. A see-through shower curtain allows light to flood the space. ➔

The Whole Family

Bathrooms fit for the entire family have to perform a lot of functions well. From offering generous storage to providing easy-care, safety-conscious surfaces, the family bath requires streamlined solutions that still leave room for a lot of activity. Flexibility, versatility, and durability are the keys to creating a bath that works for every member of the family.

bright ideas

- Hand-held showerhead and height-adjustable wall-mounted bracket
- Two-person tubs and showers
- Childproof latches on some cabinets
- Built-in hampers

This small downstairs bath gets a lot of use from the entire family—as well as guests. Storage for towels was a priority; the space-saving angled cabinets offered a simple solution. The radiator cover cleverly doubles as a towel warmer or bathing suit dryer. ➲

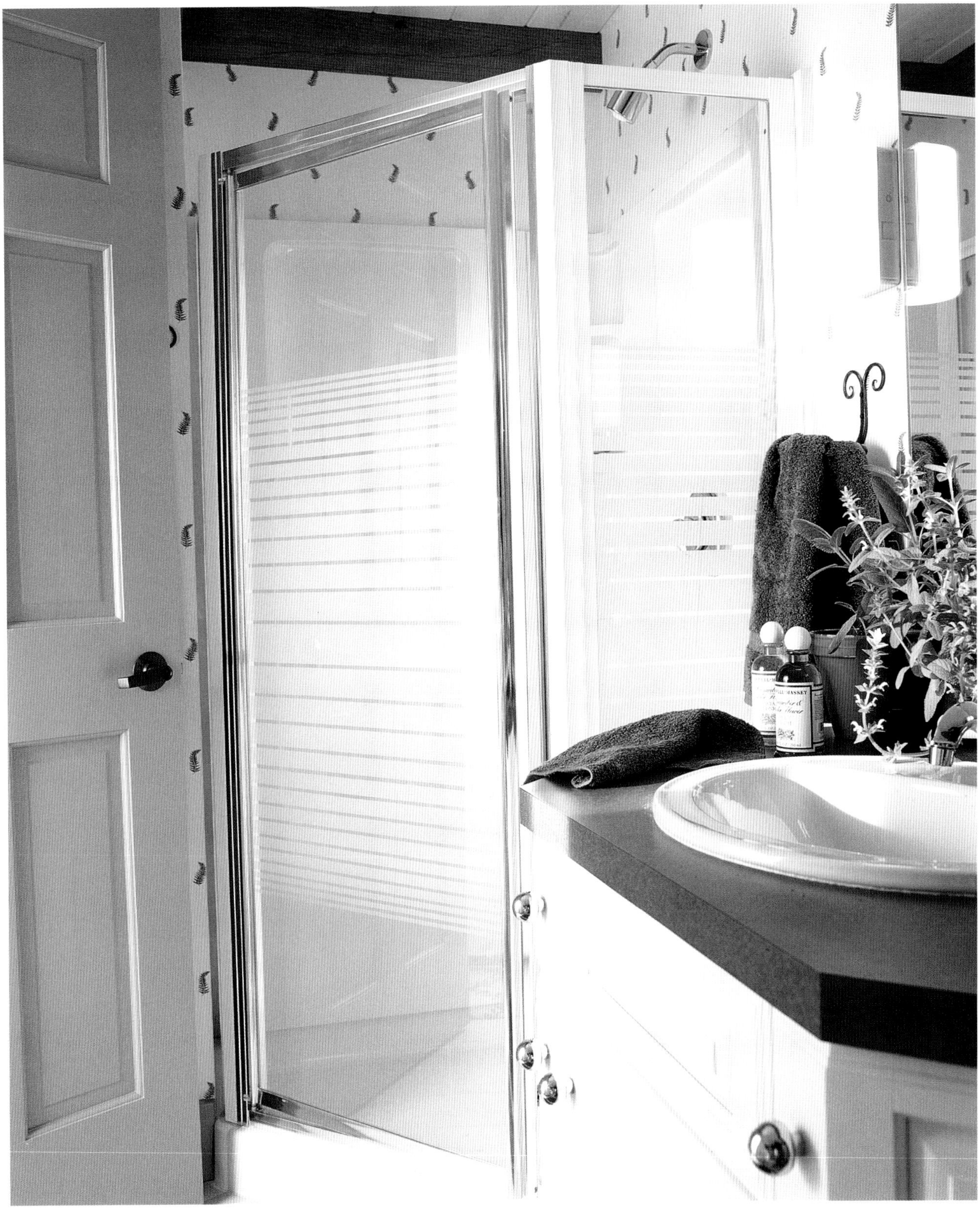

A spacious angled shower makes the most of a tight corner. ⓘ

keep in mind

Common heights of bathroom fixtures and fittings (from floor):

☐ Vanity: 36" (90cm)

☐ Shower head: 6' 7" (1.9m)

☐ Shower rod: 6' 7" (1.9m)

☐ Toilet paper holder: 24" (60cm)

☐ Towel bars: 48" (1.2m)

☐ Toothbrush holder: 48" (1.2m)

☐ Soap holder: 48" (1.2m)

☐ Tub deck height: 18" (45cm)

A glassed-in shower is oversized for easy access and features several family-friendly solutions: a tiled bench runs the length of the wall, corner shelves help organize bath amenities, and towel bars are within easy reach. ➲

Ceramic tiles with shell accents frame a mirrored medicine cabinet that provides extensive storage above the sink.

The goal of this family bathroom was to maximize storage while leaving enough room for users to move around easily. A custom built-in vanity has angled corners to minimize its impact on the floor space while providing ample storage for everything from towels to toys. ⟳

Storage beneath the room's window includes a hamper, shelves, and a platform that swings down to place a scale at floor level. ➲

Room for Two

Sharing a bathroom with a spouse or sibling doesn't mean dividing everything down the **middle**. Some important questions answered up front will help you design a bathroom that's just right for **two** (or more). Do you need one sink or two? Should you share a counter or not? If you decide on separate vanities, should they be installed at different heights? There are clever ways to make **sharing** a bathroom comfortable for all—including storage solutions to ensure that there's not too much sharing going on.

Note how the simple theme of repeating squares—the white tiles, the black accent tiles, and the windows—makes a dramatic design statement.

T*wo curvaceous pedestal sinks with shapely faucets are a handsome solution for this master bath. A glass shelf above the sinks links the his-and-her medicine cabinets and provides a surface for toothbrushes—or a pretty vase.* ➲

In this master bath, two sinks share a vanity. The sinks have been placed far enough apart to allow for a wide expanse of countertop. A storage unit with two drawers is centered beneath the counter for easy access from either sink. ☊

plan ahead

- ☐ Strive to suit separate spaces to individual needs
- ☐ Create a sink alcove with twin recessed medicine cabinets on the side walls
- ☐ Separate toilet and tub from sink area
- ☐ His and hers shower niches (be sure to measure containers first!)

Though they opted for separate sinks, this couple shares a sense of style, from the unfitted vanities to the elegant washbasins and floating faucets. Simple oval mirrors hang in front of each station while a long, narrow window above unites the two spaces.

Smart planning went into this space-saving bathroom design, in which a cleverly constructed triangle provides two distinct walls for mounting a pair of sinks. It also creates a convenient surface to keep toiletries and cosmetics nearby. ⌒

This all-white master bath makes up for the lack of storage that comes with pedestal sinks by featuring not two but three "vanities" and oversized medicine cabinets. The cabinets between the sinks are shared, while those on either side are strictly off limits. Note the towel bars hung discreetly on the sides of the his-and-hers cabinets. ➲

Consider adding chests of drawers—built-in or freestanding—a great way to keep bathroom accessories well organized.

The sink in this retro-style bathroom is shared, while the drawers, which sit on tile pedestals set on either side of the sink, create two distinct work and storage areas. The tile used on the floor, walls, and around the windows also forms the countertops on the drawers, helping to unify the room. ↻

A modern pedestal sink is the perfect solution for this clean, unadorned master bathroom. His-and-hers racks on either side of the sink keep towels handy, while a freestanding cupboard in natural wood provides needed storage. ➲

Divided Baths

If it's increased **functionality** you're after, a popular—and effective—solution is to separate the sink area from the bath and toilet, especially when multiple family members are likely to want the bathroom at the **same time**. If distinct rooms are not an option, there are still creative ways to divide a space into two or more efficient areas. For example, a well-placed wall can create a bathing area and increase **privacy**. Also, dividing a bathroom presents interesting architectural opportunities.

In this chrome and glass bath, a sandblasted glass panel separates the sink area from the toilet without sacrificing light—or style. ❍

This minimal but luxurious bathroom makes good use of natural dividers. The placement of the oversized tub between the outside wall and the glassed-in shower creates a bathing alcove with room to dress and hang a robe. ↻

Glass-paneled pocket doors separate the bathtub from the dressing area in this lavish bathroom. Pocket doors maximize both floor and wall space because they disappear into the wall: a simple solution worth remembering. ○

plan ahead

- ☐ Divide into zones by function
- ☐ Incorporate existing walls and architectural elements
- ☐ Design entrance transition area
- ☐ Create alcoves around a central space
- ☐ Vary ceiling heights to create separation

A half wall created with the same tile used on the walls serves as an effective divider without obstructing the natural light flowing in through a pair of windows. ↻

A wall separating the sink and vanity from the tub area features a simple, square cutout that adds visual interest and lets natural light pass through. It's a solution that's also an architectural statement. ◐

A supporting wall and adjacent frosted glass divider serve to define distinct areas in this bathroom. The boxy vanity seems almost to float in space, while the curve of the sink softens the angles of the room. ➲

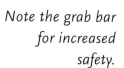

Note the grab bar for increased safety.

A cool blue-tiled partition serves as a wall to mount the sink, faucet, and mirror while creating a unique shower space behind it. ➲

Home Spas

As the world outside has become more demanding and fast-paced, we have begun to seek relaxation and rejuvenation at home, and the bathroom has been transformed into a home spa. Providing a **pampering** and restorative environment is the key. Whirlpool tubs and feature-filled showers are the fixtures most often chosen for a home spa, but there is no end to the list of amenities that can turn your bathroom into a **private** retreat. Start with a wish list and then review your budget.

bright ideas

- Steam shower or multiple-head shower
- Radiant heat in the floor
- Sauna alcove
- Heat lamps recessed into ceiling (with built-in timers)
- Towel warmers

This serene and light-filled home spa has an open shower with a showerhead that puts out a drenching, wide-angled stream. The simple design of the room and the soothing colors enhance the meditative atmosphere. ➲

The half-walls demarcate the different areas of the bathroom without closing in any of the space; the top of the wall also serves as a handy ledge.

A modern interpretation of a trough sink rests on simple wood slats that are echoed in the mirror above. The look is clean and functional. ☊

Stepped granite ledges around the whirlpool tub provide plenty of room for toiletries and towels. Chipping the edges adds textural interest, as well. ➲

Style is in the details: note the modern lines of the chrome fixtures.

The glass-walled shower enhances the room's feeling of spaciousness—nowhere are you hemmed in.

When you walk into this luxurious master bath, the cares of the world outside are sure to fade away. Amenities include a walk-in shower and a large whirlpool tub. Don't underestimate the relaxing effect of plenty of floor space to move around in. ◖

For a small bathroom, a deep soaking tub is a wonderful alternative to a large whirlpool. Zen-inspired, this tub is lined with teak and faced with granite. ◑

In a large bathroom, decorative flourishes create an atmosphere of opulence. Here, custom tiles create a border for the large mirror above the his-and-hers vanities, while adorning the floor between them is a mosaic-tiled "carpet." Details like this add up to a stylish room that's still extremely functional. 🎧

Inset into the mirror, a window lets in sunshine; recessed spots illuminate the counter from above.

The spa-like tub is accented by matte-glazed white and cream ceramic tiles on its steps and a recessed arch tiled with random color insets. ☊

Wide and shallow, the steps are easy to navigate and offer a resting spot for towels.

This luxurious bathroom features a walk-in steam shower and large rounded tub recessed into a site-built platform. The generous marble tub surround creates a perfect surface on which to rest a book or bath amenities. ↻

A heated towel rack provides an everyday indulgence.

Custom-built cabinetry in a classical style fills one wall and holds two sinks plus ample storage. A vanity takes up the short wall, offering a separate spot for primping. ☊

An open design was chosen for this home spa, making the most of the room's long, narrow proportions. A deep soaking tub flows directly into the roomy shower as light floods in from a generous window. 🎧

A simple, translucent piece of glass serves to contain shower spray.

A walk-in shower is tiled from floor to ceiling, while
a small window lets in light and a bit of fresh air.
Other smart spa-like solutions include a wall niche
for toiletries and a convenient corner perch.

Lighting & Ventilation

Lighting and ventilation are vital concerns in every bathroom. There is no overstating the importance of **good lighting** for a mirrored vanity, and proper lighting is equally essential to illuminate the tub and shower areas. Lighting also creates **ambience**. The flow of air in a bathroom is another important consideration. Mechanical ventilation is necessary to remove moisture and must be planned in advance, while fresh **air** from a well-placed window is always welcome.

bright ideas

▶ Timer to automatically shut off fan

▶ Dimmer switches allow control over brightness

▶ Accent lighting to emphasize an object or surface

Light fixtures can make bold design statements. This custom light has been incorporated into the wall, where its geometric shape echoes the angular architecture of the bathroom. ➲

An expanse of windows stretching the length of this tub admits plenty of natural light into this bathroom. Bottom-mounted blinds are sufficiently opaque to provide privacy but still allow light through, while the open top half offers treetop views. ◖

Through the sandblasted glass door lies a walk-in shower with two shower-heads and two body washers.

This commodious tub has been perfectly placed to take advantage of the natural beauty just outside the window. Fresh air and natural light combine to make for a relaxing and restoring bath.

The circular window is the focal point of this small, minimally designed bathroom, letting in natural light. ↺

A sheer shower curtain allows light to flow through.

A wide mirror maximizes the light.

Two small "cubby" windows allow shower users to control the flow of fresh air—and enhance the feeling of communing with nature. ⬆

Generous windows set high on the wall and glass doors that open to a sky-lit shower allow natural light to flood this ensuite bath. Two pinpoint spots mounted on the wall above the vanity illuminate the countertop at night. ➲

Spanning the width of the room, the mirror maximizes the light, as does the use of pale and light-reflective materials: maple cabinets, stainless-steel sinks, polished-chrome faucets, and limestone vanity and floor tiles. The mirror's glass sconces were sandblasted to eliminate glare. ↻

Ventilation can be discreet: this small duct routes moist air to the outside of the house.

Opaque glass for the bifold windows screens bathers from view while admitting light.

An abundance of light in this bathroom led to the invention of a simple but creative solution: a grid of brick that allows fresh air to flow into the bathroom but preserves privacy. ➲

The use of light pine throughout the bathroom and a unique woven ceiling combine for a simple, clean look.

This bathroom has plenty of natural and artificial light. Wall sconces illuminate the twin mirrors above the long vanity and a ceiling fixture shines down on the tub for nighttime bathing. ☊

![pencil icon]

keep
in mind

☐ A fan should have a cubic feet per minute (CFM) rating high enough to change air in the bathroom 8 times per hour

☐ Calculate cubic footage of room and divide by 7.5 to find approximate CFM rating needed

☐ Fan noise levels are measured in sones; look for units that generate no more than 6.5 sones (ultra-quiet fans produce less than 1.5 sones)

Wall-mounted lighting at eye level on both sides of the mirror is ideal for the vanity. Here, voluptuous sconces illuminate the face while softening some of the hard edges of the room. ☍

Natural Bath

s much as it is a cleansing **ritual**, the bath is also an opportunity for relaxation and restoration: savvy bathroom designers know that a glimpse of nature can help soothe both **body and soul.** Whether your bath looks out on awe-inspiring natural scenery, your own backyard garden, or the treetops in the distance, consider ways you can bring the outdoors in.

plan ahead

☐ One well-placed window is better than two without views

☐ Position shower to take advantage of window view, too

☐ Window seats offer a pleasant resting spot

Softly draped fabric blinds can be raised to flood the room with sunlight or lowered to create an intimate ambience.

A freestanding tub rests atop a pedestal in the midst of the tropical plants and warm wood that make up this exotic bath oasis.

A wrap-around window adds architectural interest
and offers a panoramic view, making this rounded
tub an excellent spot from which to contemplate
nature. The long, narrow window admits plenty of
natural light, too. ☝

One of the glass panels is sandblasted for added privacy while the other frames the view.

Wood, stone, and glass are the elements of this artfully simple bathroom, designed to show off the beauty of the woodsy setting. ⮰

Bring nature indoors: given light and moisture, many plants will grow happily in a bathroom.

This bathroom comes close to erasing the line between indoors and out. An entire wall of glass opens out into a private, fenced-in garden. The shower, bordered only by transparent glass (including the doors), allows users to experience the feeling of getting "back to nature" as fully as possible while still being indoors. ⮰

Opening onto a private terrace, this serene bath features expanses of smooth stone. A restrained use of extraneous details leaves bathers free to concentrate on the relaxing view. ➲

A simple stone slab serves as a ledge for bath amenities.

A soaring vaulted ceiling frames the views of hilltops and blue sky outside this magnificent bath. The liberal use of stone evokes the surrounding environment, while glass blocks at the bathing level preserve privacy. ⊙

While modest in its proportions, this bath was designed to take advantage of the view on three sides, creating a bathing oasis that opens to the outdoors. A soaking tub encourages relaxation and contemplation while an adjacent shower also allows enjoyment of the view. ⌒

In this tropical setting, bathing takes place overlooking a lush private garden. The design of the tub and simple accessories set the mood for a meditative bath. Opt for earthy materials and lots of greenery to create your own tropical bath. ➲

Experimenting with Style

The bathroom is an ideal room for exploring new decorating territory. It can extend the decorative **themes** used in other rooms of the home or be a place to experiment with new looks. Flooring, countertops, cabinetry, and fixtures can all be used as **expressions** of style. Whether you're starting from scratch or preparing to freshen up an existing bathroom, there is a wide range of materials and accessories available to spark your creativity.

Bright Ideas

▶ Embellish with moldings and trims

▶ Mix and match hardware styles

▶ Experiment with borders for tile floors

▶ Style is in the details: think switch plates and doorknobs

A long, narrow bathroom adjoining the master bedroom makes a retro modern statement with a wall of sleek cabinetry and a freestanding vanity. Color is used sparingly, but to dramatic effect, on the mosaic wall. ↻

Surprise is an element of style, too: an ornately framed mirror adds to the eclectic look. ⌢

The triangular shape of the wall-mounted toilet provides a dynamic contrast to the curvaceous light fixtures.

Look to accessories to make a statement: the soap dish and toothbrush holder are supremely stylish, yet fully functional.

For a modern look, opt for one or two materials and keep details to a bare minimum. In this sleek bathroom, wood and chrome set the tone. The handsome pedestal sink is a focal point, while the chrome faucet complements the hardware and accessories. ◑

Experiment with textures and materials to create a unique look. This bathroom features walls of tempered glass and a counter made of a poured stone commonly used for laboratory tables. The pale hue of the glass and the warm wooden floor help to soften the effect. ➲

Extending the color palette of the master bedroom into the bath, this room features neutral shades of cream and taupe, accented by black. The textured wallcovering introduces an extra touch of subtle elegance. ⊂

The patterned fabric of the chair is reflected in the black tile square inset into the white floor.

Comfort is as welcome in the bathroom as it is in other areas of the home. An upholstered chair and a cushioned bench offer welcoming spots to relax. ⋂

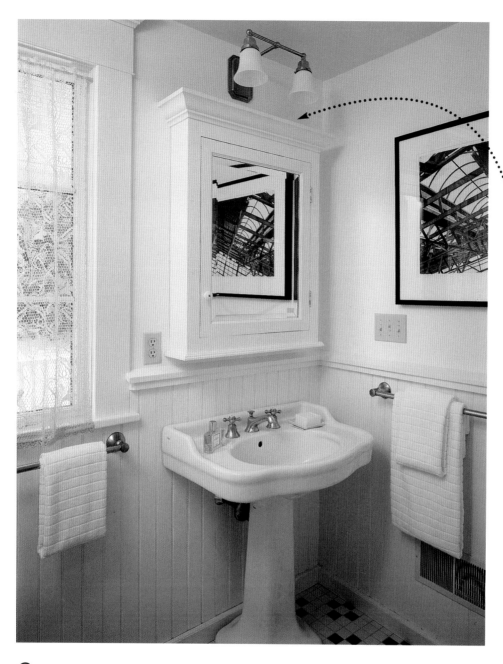

Architectural moldings around the window are echoed on the medicine cabinet, enhancing the traditional ambience.

Note the accent lighting that highlights the ceiling cutouts.

Choose timeless fixtures and decorative details for classic elegance: a pedestal sink, traditional hardware, a wall-mounted medicine cabinet, bead board walls, and plenty of white. ⊙

Mixing styles can yield striking results, as in this bathroom, where a traditional pedestal sink is perfectly at home surrounded by modern forms and finishes. A trio of architectural shelves serves as a functional backdrop for a mirror mounted in a bold green frame. ➲

Storage Solutions

hether you're designing a **new** bathroom or renovating an existing one, factor as much storage into your plans as possible. Larger bathrooms have a leg up, but with a little creativity—and planning—smaller bathrooms can find **clever** ways to take advantage of every square inch of space. There's no such thing as too much storage, and smart solutions will enhance the functionality and **efficiency** of your bathroom.

bright ideas

- Wire shelves permit ventilation and are easy to clean
- Pegs, hooks, and baskets are ideal for kids' stuff
- Drawer dividers offer hidden organization
- Closet shelves that pull out for easy access

Though small, this bathroom is a true marriage of style and substance, with an assortment of drawers, ledges, and shelves forming an abstract sculpture of useful storage. ➲

Storage options in this elegant master bathroom abound. The built-in cabinetry makes maximum use of the vertical space and combines drawers, cupboards, and open shelving to create a storage unit that holds everything from linens to toiletries. ⊙

A roll-top "garage" hides sink-side clutter.

Vented cabinets on either side serve as hampers.

A handsome, Arts-and-Crafts inspired storage unit serves as a vanity and more. Making full use of the available space, the custom-built unit stretches from floor to ceiling. Accessible shelves keep fresh towels within arm's reach of the tub; substantial storage space exists behind closed doors. ☊

A spacious, unusually shaped bathroom takes full advantage of the square footage. A pair of elegant marble-topped wooden vanities, with both drawers and cupboards, flank a taller five-drawer shared cabinet.

Tranquility reigns in this small but well-organized bathroom. The pale hues of the poured-in-place concrete counters and tub are echoed in the bleached maple cabinets, which feature two rows of drawers. Drawers are a good option in a bathroom with limited space, as they are easier to organize and can often store more than cupboards. ◓

In a bathroom of modest proportions, smart solutions make a big difference. This pullout cabinet packs a lot of storage into a narrow vertical space that might otherwise go unused. Everything from toiletries to bathroom appliances can be kept handy yet can also be quickly hidden away. ➲

Bars keep items in place.

Simplicity is the goal of this bathroom, where smooth surfaces and a neutral palette call for sleek storage solutions. The extended vanity serves as a stylish base for the concrete countertops while providing both open and hidden storage. ◓

The medicine chest rests atop a pedestal that also hides the plumbing.

Exposed pipes and a textured concrete countertop give this bathroom style; a substantial built-in cupboard with two open shelves provides storage. ☊

This grab bar marries style and safety.

plan ahead

☐ Recess shallow shelving between wall studs

☐ Annex adjacent bedroom closet for more storage space

☐ Relocate linen closet to hall or bedroom

Storage can be more than merely functional; it can add visual interest and style to a room. A vertical niche created from marble tiles becomes a focal point and keeps towels within arm's reach. ℂ

Smart solution: take advantage of the surface created by the built-out cabinet to install a hook.

A mirror above the sink did not allow for a traditional medicine cabinet in this bathroom, but a cabinet fit nicely against the adjacent wall, providing a convenient place to stow towels and other daily essentials. ☊

The countertop in this bathroom extends the length of the room and uses different widths to create useful surfaces without taking up too much floor space. A double cabinet above the toilet serves as a medicine cabinet. ☊

To accommodate the window in this large master bathroom, the his-and-hers vanity had to be split in two. Ample storage underneath each station keeps personal items separate while a low banquette bridges the two areas and provides communal storage and a place to rest. ◑

An oversized recessed medicine cabinet is a smart solution for this bathroom with twin pedestal sinks. Storage is easily accessible yet doesn't crowd the sinks or interfere with faucets. ➲

Smart & Accessible Design

One measure of **good bath design** is how well it accommodates users of all ages, sizes, and abilities. The goal should be to create a bathroom with as few barriers and obstacles as possible. Safety measures such as **grab bars** benefit everyone, plus there are a host of conveniences that simply make a bathroom more **efficient** and enjoyable to use. Thinking ahead about who uses the bathroom—and how they use it—is a good place to start.

bright ideas

▶ Grab bars

▶ Slip-resistant surfaces

▶ In-shower seating

There are many different types of fixed showerheads available today, able to deliver specific kinds of spray.

An ornately tiled niche holds shampoo and other necessities at an easily accessible height, at once more convenient and safer than trying to balance everything on the edge or in the corners of the bathtub. ⋂

This bath is an example of a happy partnership of old-fashioned style and modern conveniences. An early twentieth century tub and faucets are joined by a new hand-held showerhead, bringing bathing up to date. Hand-held showerheads allow users of very different heights to easily share a shower. (They're also great for rinsing out the tub.) ⊂

A heated towel rack—placed within arm's reach of the tub—is one of the most practical and delightful amenities that can be easily added to a bathroom. ☊

This tub sports a hand-held spray nozzle to facilitate rinsing.

A shower bench is a convenient and smart addition to any shower, especially a steam shower that encourages lingering. ⊃

Sturdy chrome-plated hinges allow the bench to swing up against the wall when not in use.

Mount a shaving mirror above the sink to make a morning ritual more comfortable and pleasant. No more leaning over the countertop! ⊂

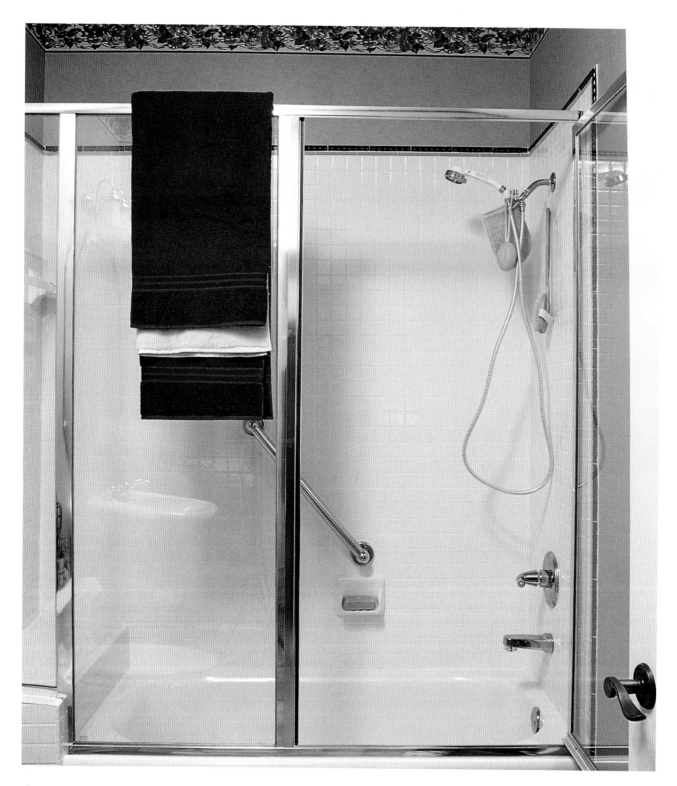

Safety features can be easily built in—this bathroom features a grab bar and tiled bench, while a hand-held showerhead is convenient for users of all ages. ◖

keep in mind

☐ Side mounted faucets are easy to reach

☐ Single-lever controls are easy to grasp

☐ Shower doors always swing out

☐ Tubs should be set into decks wide enough to sit on comfortably and safely

☐ Standard toilet height is 14.5" to 15" (36 to 38cm), up to 18" (45cm) for taller people

A light-filled bathroom commands a stunning view, and shows off several stylish and smart solutions. The stone tub surround is an elegant choice and is wide enough for sitting, making it easy to move in and out of the bath. Built-in bars offer additional security. ⊂

Unfitted Cabinetry

Vanities that look like freestanding pieces of furniture (even though they may be secured to the wall) are a simple way to add old-world charm and flexibility to a bathroom. An antique piece can be retrofitted with a new basin—or a new piece that simply looks old may do the trick. Other freestanding furniture is also welcome in the bathroom. Think about incorporating a vintage armoire or chest of drawers for an eclectic look.

bright ideas

- Turn an antique washstand into a vanity
- A leggy piece will open up a small space
- Freestanding furniture offers flexible storage
- Pair a vanity with an antique medicine cabinet

A freestanding sink makes ingenious use of the curved wall space in a small, renovated bath. The rustic hand-hewn wood surface is counterbalanced by the whimsical elegance of the legs. ➲

A basic white basin has been set into a distressed wood table base and paired with a tall, matching mirror for an antique look. ☺

Traditionally styled cherry cabinets evoke an antique washstand and are complemented by a counter and backsplash with the look of granite. ↻

Details like ornate drawer pulls and claw feet add to the charm.

An antique dresser with a curved front has been fitted with a simple white basin for a charming country bath. The brass faucets, hardware, and accessories complement the warm wood and complete the traditional look. ➲

Freestanding pieces are both practical and decorative. In this bathroom, a pine cupboard provides much-needed storage. Its glass compartments keep items on view and help the piece to fit in unobtrusively. ☊

The bottom section, with wooden doors, offers discreet storage.

A pine wardrobe lends its imposing presence to a handsomely outfitted bathroom, providing ample storage— and style. ➲

A simple antique washstand placed next to the tub provides a convenient place to rest towels while adding old-world charm. With a drawer and a lower level shelf, this single piece packs a lot of storage into a small space. ◓

Converted Baths

The appeal of an **extra** bathroom is undeniable, though finding the space for it may mean converting another room or unused space. Beyond the obvious plumbing issues, there may be **special** challenges: tight corners to negotiate, wide open spaces that need to be filled, or an awkwardly placed window to conceal. The nice thing about a converted bathroom is that an unusual space presents an opportunity to explore **exciting** solutions.

Unused space on the third-floor was converted into a bath that has old-world charm but is not lacking for space. Bead board on the walls and ceilings was stained a warm tone. The bright white trim is a nice contrast to the wood and offsets the classic pedestal sink. ➲

plan ahead

☐ Place a stone slab underneath the toilet when floors are wood

☐ Take advantage of sloping walls/ceilings to create clever storage

☐ Bring in a comfortable chair when space permits

A small bedroom became a romantic country bathroom. To protect the woodwork, the floors received extra coatings of varnish, and bead board was added around the tub to guard against splashing. ⚏

An attic bathroom makes its unusual dimensions work. Windows fill one wall and bring in natural light, while ceiling fixtures illuminate the room at night. ➲

Classic Revival

I f you prefer older or **antique** bathroom styles, there is no reason even in this age of technological marvels not to indulge your old-fashioned leanings. A classic pedestal sink or claw foot tub can make a **beautiful** focal point for a room or serve as an interesting counterpoint to more **modern touches**. Both salvaged pieces and new ones modeled after the classics are readily available. Remember: a classic never goes out of style.

Among the most popular designs ever, the classic pedestal sink remains a favorite. In this country house bathroom, it has been paired with a distressed table that serves as both a convenient resting place for necessities and a display area for found objects. The bead board and traditional mirror complete the look of this timeless bathroom. ☊

Note the tub tray, a simple solution when there is no tub surround.

An antique claw foot tub is wide and deep, perfect for a long, relaxing soak. Hardware that is old-fashioned in style but modern in function is the best bet. ☊

A chunky pedestal sink with extra curves on the corners is paired with antique mirror and sconces for a shabby chic look. A glass shelf and wall-mounted toothbrush and towel holders make up for the lack of counter space. ⟲

A modern walk-in shower adds to the amenities without diminishing the style.

An antique slipper tub is the centerpiece of this all-white bathroom. Vintage mirrors reflect the light and a stool with elegant legs sits to one side, while a collection of lady head vases overlooks the tub. ➲

A voluptuous antique sink provides a dramatic focal point for this otherwise simple bathroom. Note the original hardware and curvaceous turned legs. ◐

An unusually shaped pedestal sink makes a strong retro statement. Just above, a niche offers a bit of open storage while the recessed cabinet reveals additional shelves. ↻

Whether antique or reproduction, traditional hardware completes a classic look.

Antiques from earlier eras continue to inspire modern interpretations. New classics like this luxurious tub with chrome faucet and handheld showerhead offer today's functionality with a nod to the visual pleasures of days past. ↻

Bathroom Planning Resources

Worksheets

When you are planning a new bathroom or remodeling an existing one, it's a good idea to take a few minutes to think about the room in the context of your home and life. The National Kitchen and Bath Association suggests creating a bath planning worksheet that includes the following information:

▶ Who will use the bathroom?

▶ How many people will use the bathroom at one time?

▶ What activities will take place in the bathroom (makeup application, bathing, hair care, dressing, exercise, laundry, other)?

▶ Do you prefer the toilet and/or bidet to be isolated from the other fixtures?

▶ Would you like his and hers facilities?

▶ Do you need a closet as part of the new bathroom?

▶ What type of style would you like the new bathroom to have— country, traditional, vintage, etc.?

▶ What is your budget range?

▶ When do you want to start?

▶ When do you realistically want to complete the project?

▶ How long will you own the home—is it a short- or long-term investment?

▶ Is return on investment a primary concern?

▶ Do you plan on moving out and renting the residence in the future?

▶ What features do you like about your current bathrooms?

Another good planning tool is a checklist to help you determine what features and amenities you absolutely need versus ones that would be nice to have. Then you can allocate your budget accordingly.

Feature	Need	Want
New vanity	☐	☐
Separate shower	☐	☐
Spa-type shower	☐	☐
Shower door	☐	☐
Sinks for two	☐	☐
Tubs for two	☐	☐
Whirlpool tub	☐	☐
New toilet	☐	☐
Bidet	☐	☐
Linen storage	☐	☐
Additional storage	☐	☐
Exercise area	☐	☐
Lighting fixtures	☐	☐
Heat lamp	☐	☐
New floor	☐	☐
New wall surfaces	☐	☐
New countertops	☐	☐
Heated towel bar	☐	☐
Custom cabinetry	☐	☐
Mirrors	☐	☐
Makeup/Shaving mirror	☐	☐
Ventilation	☐	☐
Electrical outlets	☐	☐

Information and Products

If you are interested in hiring a qualified professional, here is a list of design and planning resources to help with the design of your bathroom:

American Institute of Architects (AIA)—When making structural changes, an architect should be considered. Many, but not all, architects belong to The American Institute of Architects. Call (202) 626-7300 for information and the phone number of your local chapter. www.aiaonline.com

The American Society of Interior Designers (ASID)—An interior designer can provide helpful advice especially when remodeling an existing space. The American Society of Interior Designers represents over 20,000 professionally qualified interior designers. Call ASID's client/referral service at (800) 775-ASID. www.asid.org

The National Kitchen and Bath Association (NKBA)—The National Kitchen and Bath Association Web site is an excellent general resource for information about bathroom design: www.nkba.com. For more information, write NKBA, 687 Willow Grove Street, Hackettstown, NJ 07840 or call (800) 401-NKBA, extension 665

National Association of the Remodeling Industry (NARI)—When it's time to select a contractor to work on your bathroom project, you might consider a member of the National Association of the Remodeling Industry. Call (800) 611-6274 for more information. www.nari.org

National Association of Home Builders (NAHB)—When you're looking at builders to construct a new home, contact the National Association of Home Builders. Call (800) 368-5242 for more information. www.nahb.org

The following manufacturers, associations and resources may be helpful as you plan your bathroom:

FLOORING

Italian Trade Commission
Ceramic Tile Department
499 Park Avenue
New York NY 10022
(212) 980-1500
www.italtrade.com

Trade Commission of Spain
Ceramic Tile Department
2655 Le Jeune Road, Suite 114
Coral Gables, FL 33134
(305) 446-4387
www.tilespain.com

www.floorfacts.com
(a global directory that helps
   consumers explore flooring
   options)

LIGHTING

American Lighting Association
P.O. Box 420288
Dallas, TX 75342-0288
(800) 274-4484
www.americanlightingassoc.
   com

UNIVERSAL DESIGN

Center for Universal Design
North Carolina State University
Box 8613
Raleigh, NC 27695-8613
(800) 647-6777
www.design.ncsu.edu/cud

Universal Designers &
   Consultants
6 Grant Avenue
Takoma Park, MD 20912
301 270 2470
www.universaldesign.com

Adaptive Environments
374 Congress Street,
   Suite 301
Boston, MA 02210
(617) 695-1225
www.adaptenv.org

PAINT

Benjamin Moore
(800) 6-PAINT 6
www.benjaminmoore.com
Pratt & Lambert
www.prattandlambert.com

Sherwin-Williams
(800) 474-3794
www.sherwin-williams.com

FAUCETS/FIXTURES/ SHOWERS/TUBS/ ACCESSORIES

Many of these manufacturers offer a full range of bath products while others specialize in specific product areas. All are good resources for information.

American Standard
(800) 524-9797
www.americanstandard-us.
   com

Aqua Glass
(901) 632-2501
www.aquaglass.com

Broadway
(800) 766-1966
www.broadwaycollection.com

Delta
(800) 345-DELTA
www.deltafaucet.com

Grohe
(630) 582-7711
www.grohe.com

Jacuzzi
(925) 938-7411
www.jacuzzi.com

Jado
(800) 227-2734
www.jado.com

Jason
(800) 255-5766
www.jasonint.com

Kohler
(800) 4-KOHLER
www.kohlerco.com

Lasco
(800) 877-2005
www.lascobathware.com

Moen
(800) BUY-MOEN
www.moen.com

Mr. Steam
(800) 72/76-STEAM
www.sussmanlifestylegroup.
   com

Myson
(802) 654-7500
www.mysoninc.com

Newport Brass
(714) 436-0805
www.newportbrass.com

Price Pfister
(800) 732-8238
www.pricepfister.com

Runtal
(800) 526-2621
www.runtalnorthamerica.com

St. Thomas
(619) 336-3980
www.stthomascreations.com

Steamist
(201) 933-0700
www.steamist.com

Sterling
(888) STERLING
www.sterlingplumbing.com

Swan
(800) 325-7008
www.theswancorp.com

Thermasol
(800) 776-0711
www.thermasol.com

Toto
(800) 350-8686
www.totousa.com

Universal-Rundle
(800) 955-0316
www.universal-rundle.com

WINDOWS/DOORS

Andersen
(800) 426-4261
www.andersenwindows.com

Loewen
(800) 245-2295
www.loewen.com

Marvin
(800) 241-9450
www.marvin.com

Morgan
(800) 877-9482
www.morgandoors.com

Pella
(800) 54-PELLA
www.pella.com

Pozzi
(800) 257-9663
www.pozzi.com

Moen
(800) BUY MOEN
www.moen.com

Price Pfister
(800) 732-8238
www.pricepfister.com

Photo Credits

Beate Works/©Grey Crawford: p. 64

©Laurie Black: p. 92 (Architect: David Bearss, AIA; Bath design: Kathleen Donohue of Neil Kelly Signature Cabinets)

©Tom Bonner: pp. 97 left (Architect David Hertz, AIA)

©Judith Bromley: pp. 44–45 (Architect: Kathryn Quinn), 49 (Architect: Kathryn Quinn)

©Steven Brooke: pp. 28 (Architect: Barry Berkus, AIA of B3 Architects; Interior Design: Barbara Dalton, ASID), 29 (Architect: Barry Berkus, AIA of B3 Architects; Interior Design: Barbara Dalton, ASID), 35 inset (Interior Design: Ed Biggs), 56 (Interior design: Charles Riley), 56 inset (Interior design: Charles Riley), 94–95 (House design: Scholz Design; Interior Design: Slifer Designs), 114 bottom (Architect: Lee Ann Fergeson)

©Grey Crawford: pp. 40 (Architect: Steven Estreich), 96 (Designer: Charles Ward)

Elizabeth Whiting Associates/ ©Andreas von Einsiedel: p. 48; ©Rodney Hyett: pp. 22, 52 bottom, 115; ©Neil Lorimer: p. 97 right; ©Friedhelm Thomas: p. 44 left

©David Frazier: pp. 86 (Interior Design: Nancy Gales ASID of Southeastern Galleries), 87

(Interior Design: Nancy Gales ASID of Southeastern Galleries), 114 top (Interior Design: Charles Riley)

©Tria Giovan: pp. 10, 23, 26 top, 26 bottom, 52 top, 103, 107 bottom, 118, 119

©Kari Haavisto: pp. 32 (House Design: Larry W. Garnett; Interior Design: Suzanne S. Felber), 35 (Architects: Bell Larson Architects), 38 (Interior Design: Nancy D. Mullan ASID, CKD), 39 top (Interior Design: Nancy D. Mullan ASID, CKD) 35 bottom (Interior Design: Nancy D. Mullan ASID, CKD), 65 (Architect: Mark McInturff AIA), 70 (Architect: Mark McInturff AIA), 108 (House Design: Larry W. Garnett; Interior Design: Suzanne S. Felber)

©Nancy Hill: pp. 41 (Architect: Lloyd Jafvert), 60, 61, 93 (Stirling Design Associates), 102, 116, 117 top (Stirling Design Associates)

The Interior Archive/©Ken Hayden: pp. 54 (Designer: Jonathan Reed), 55 (Designer: Jonathan Reed)

©Fritz von der Schulenberg: p. 72 (Designer: Jed Johnson)

©Michael Jensen: pp. 66–67 (Prentiss Architects)

©Jessie Walker Associates: pp. 34 (Designer: Claire Golan & Associates Interior Design),

34 inset (Designer: Claire Golan & Associates Interior Design), 117 bottom (Architect: Larry Schwall/Designer: Julie McDowell), 120 left (Designer: Susan Chastain)

©Doug Kennedy: pp. 30 (Architect: Charles M. Hill; Interior Design: Katherine Stephens), 31 (Architect: Charles M. Hill; Interior Design: Katherine Stephens), 31 inset (Architect: Charles M. Hill; Interior Design: Katherine Stephens)

©Dennis Krukowski: pp. 20, 21

©davidduncanlivingston.com: pp. 24, 25, 63, 98, 99, 100, 101, 109

©Jeff McNamara: pp. 33 (House Design: Yankee Barn Homes; Interior Design: Charles Riley), 33 inset (House Design: Yankee Barn Homes; Interior Design: Charles Riley), 36 (House Design: Yankee Barn Homes; Interior Design: Charles Riley), 37 (House Design: Yankee Barn Homes; Interior Design: Charles Riley)

©Kit Morris: pp. 18 (Designer: Kathy St. Clair, CKD, CBD of Ken Topping Home Improvements), 19 (Designer: Kathy St. Clair, CKD, CBD of Ken Topping Home Improvements), 73 (Architect: Dan Phipps), 85 (Architect: Lindy Small), 122 (Designer: Kathy St. Clair, CKD, CBD of Ken Topping Home Improvements), 123 (Designer: Kathy St. Clair, CKD,

CBD of Ken Topping Home Improvements)

©Tim Street Porter: pp. 2, 11, 16, 17, 27, 57, 68, 71, 74–75, 76, 77 top, 77 bottom, 78, 79, 81, 89, 90–91, 120 right

©Mark Samu: pp. 12, 14, 15, 88, 111, 113

©Michael Skott: pp. 104 (Architect: Tom McCallum, AIA; Interior Design: Linda Humphrey), 105 (Architect: Tom McCallum, AIA; Interior Design: Linda Humphrey)

©William P. Steele: pp. 58 (Interior Design: Suzanne Felber), 59 (Interior Design: Suzanne Felber), 112 (Interior Design: Suzanne Felber)

©Brian Vanden Brink: pp. 13 (Architect: Alan Freysinger; Interior Design: Christina Oliver), 47, 84 (Architect: Scogin, Elam & Bray), 110, 121 (Architect: Scholz & Barclay)

©Dominique Vorillion: pp. 6, 8, 42–43 (Architect: Lorcan O'Herlihy), 46, 50, 51, 53 (Architect: Lorcan O'Herlihy), 62 (Architect: William Hefner), 69 (Biben/Bosley Architects), 69 inset (Architect: Biben/Bosley), 80 (Architect: Foster Meagher), 82–83 (Architect: Tim Andrews), 83 right (Architect: Tim Andrews), 106, 107 top (Interior Design Rebecca S. Shaw)

Index